# The
# Little Book of
# Incredible
# Eye-Twisters

# Eye-Twisters

# The Little Book of Incredible Eye-Twisters

metro

Published by Metro Publishing Ltd, 3 Bramber Court, 2 Bramber Road,
London W14 9PB, England

First published in paperback in 2002

ISBN 1 84358 044 6

British Library Cataloguing-in-Publication Data: A catalogue record for this book is
available from the British Library.

Design by ENVY

Printed and bound in Great Britain by William Clowes Ltd, Beccles, Suffolk
www.clowes.co.uk

9 10 11

Papers used by Metro Publishing Ltd are natural, recyclable products made from
wood grown in sustainable forests. The manufacturing processes conform to the
environmental regulations of the country of origin.

Every effort has been made to contact the copyright-holders, but some were
untraceable. We would be grateful if the relevant people would contact us.

A percentage of profits from this book will be
donated to the Sightsavers charity.

Are the two lines curved?
Are you sure?

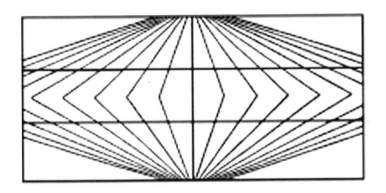

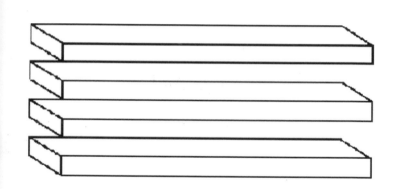

How many shelves –
three or four?

Eye-Twisters

Are you looking down the coil
from the left-hand side
or the right?

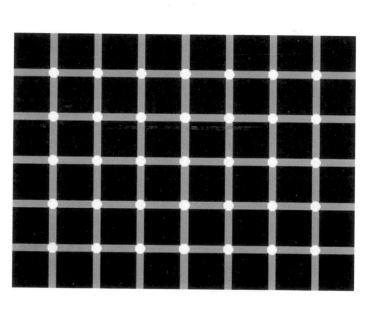

Are the dots white, or black?

Eye-Twisters

# Spot the black circles!

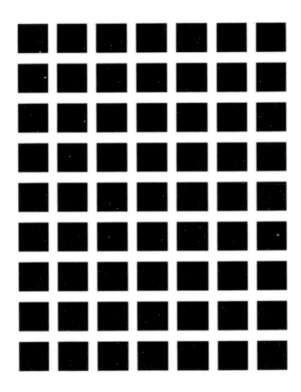

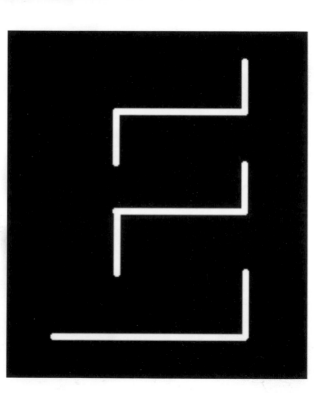

Do you see three lines,

or do you see a letter?

Lines, squares or triangles?

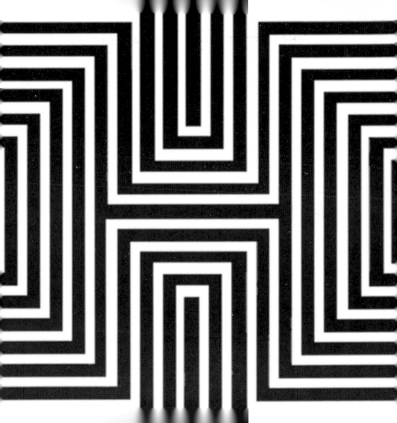

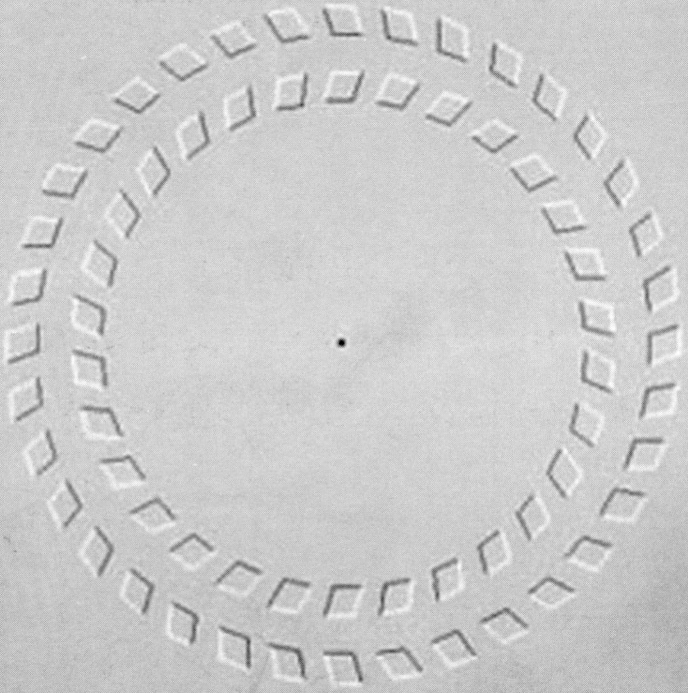

Focus on the black dot,
and move your head gently
towards the image. Spooky!

Eye-Twisters

The never-ending stairs.
These'll soon get you fit...

Eye-Twisters

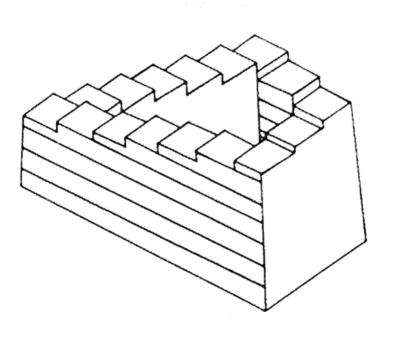

Can you see the two-dimensional image shimmering like a three-dimensional one?

# More impossible steps!

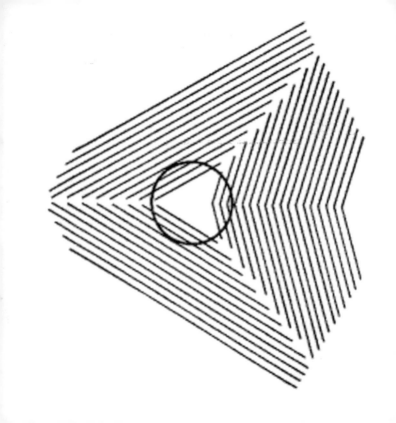

Believe it or not, that's a
circle you're looking at!

Eye-Twisters

Ladies and gentlemen,

a square with bendy lines!

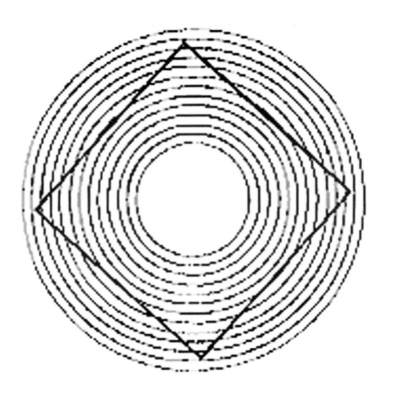

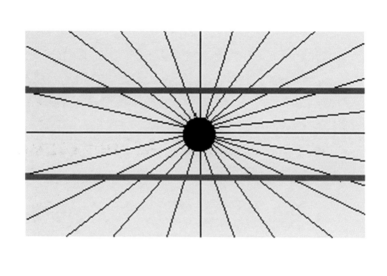

# How to make straight lines curve...

Eye-Twisters

Look into the vase.
What do you see?

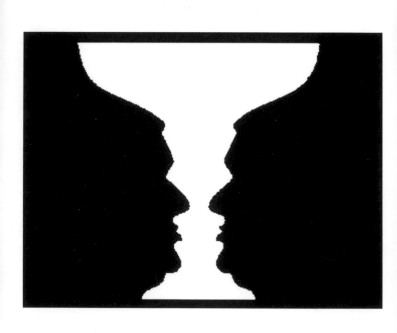

# Another magic vase!

Look at the central circles.
Which one is bigger?

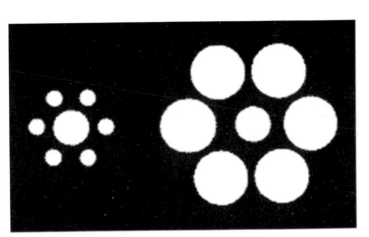

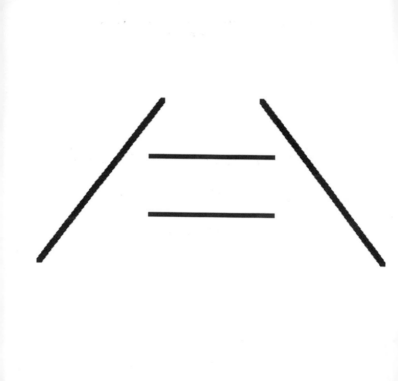

Which of the horizontal
lines is longer?
Are you sure?

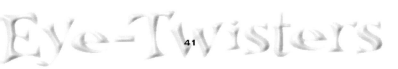

It's funny how your brain creates
things that don't exist.
Take these circles, for instance...

Eye-Twisters

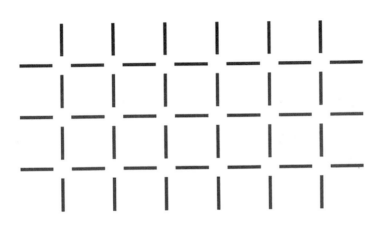

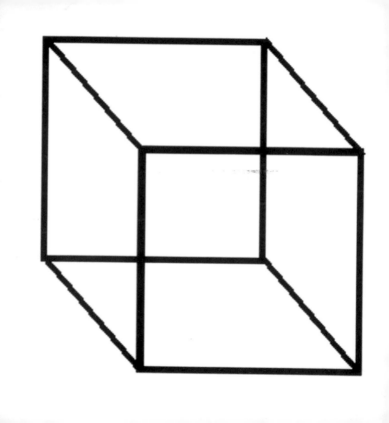

# The magic cube –
## which face is at the front?

Eye-Twisters

Are you looking at the inside
or the outside of the book?

46

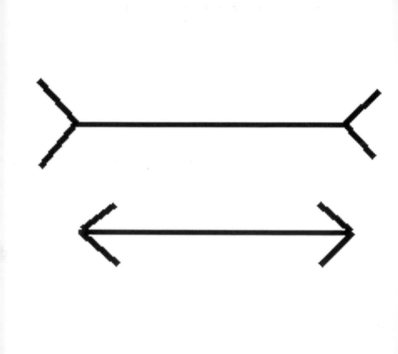

Which line is longer?
Check again!

Eye-Twisters

It's amazing how creatures

can be so alike...

Beware the curse of vanity!

# The demon drink!

Eye-Twisters

# Two devilishly beautiful women!

Which is the tallest soldier?

Eye-Twisters

Who do you see –

an old lady or a young one?

Eye-Twisters

Is this person lying
about their age?

Eye-Twisters

# Bunny Duck!

Wh'od have thought that
      Eskimos and Red Indians
could be so closely related?

Eye-Twisters

How many legs does this
elephant have?

Here's a tricky one.
Do you see an old man
surrounded by leaves, or a
couple kissing?
Don't give up – it'll come!

Eye-Twisters

A hungry bird, or a
hungry fisherman?

A very elegant
moustachioed lady.

Eye-Twisters

# Spot the dog!

See the face of Jesus.
    Stare at the four dots for
thirty seconds, then close your
    eyes and hold back your head.
Have you seen the light?

So good to see you, your Majesty.
Stare at the image for a
minute, then close your eyes.

Eye-Twisters

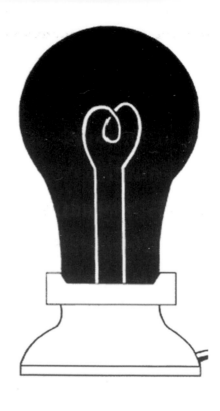

Let there be light!

Stare at the image for a
minute, then shut your eyes...

Eye-Twisters

Lady in black.
Stare at the image for a minute and then close your eyes...

Eye-Twisters

I

LOVE

PARIS IN THE

THE SPRINGTIME

Read the sign.

Now read it again.

Were you right first time?

Eye-Twisters

Rearrange the sections
of the top image, and you
get the bottom image.
Where does the hole
come from?

Eye-Twisters

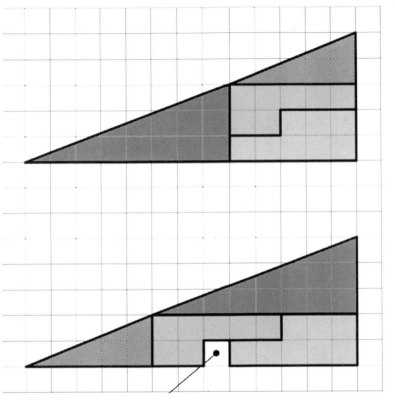